QUARAN TEAM

To order additional copies of this book, contact:
Xlibris
844-714-8691
www.Xlibris.com
Orders@Xlibris.com

ISBN: Softcover   978-1-6698-3585-1
        Hardcover   978-1-6698-3586-8
        EBook   978-1-6698-3584-4

Print information available on the last page

Rev. date: 06/30/2022

QUARAN TEAM

HAIKU

LINDA KOHLER BARNES

AUTHOR & ARTIST

Quaran Team

Author & Artist
Linda Kohler Barnes

Written pages include:

Title
"Scientific name"
Haiku

MOOSE WEAR A MASK
(Moosu thinkimornow)

EARLY IN THE MORN

THINKING, QUIETLY AT HOME

THE WHOLE WORLD HAS CHANGED

HARE I GO

(Lepus weramaskme)

NOT COMFY AT ALL

WEARING A MASK EVERYWHERE

IT'S STUFFY OUTSIDE

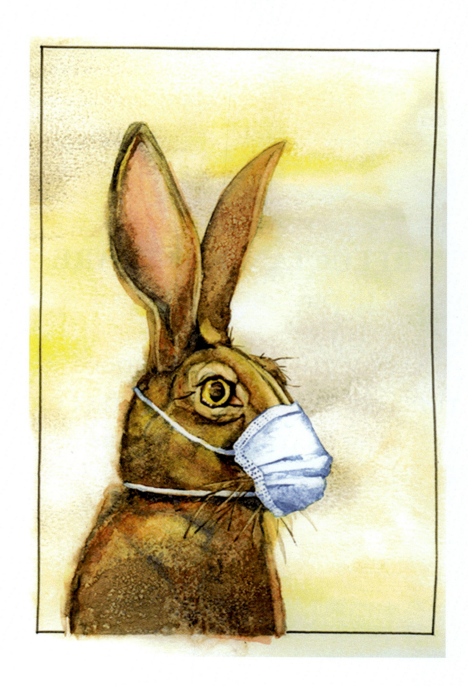

RELUCTANT TO SHARE
(Rattus hoardericuss)

STOCKPILING SCARCE GOODS

THINKING THEY'RE THE SMARTEST ONES

PACKRATS ARE HOARDERS

IN CONFINEMENT
(Loxodonta windowwatchi)

STAYING SAFE AT HOME

THE WORLD IS OUT THE WINDOW

THANKFUL FOR HEROES

BLOW IT OUR YER BOMBARDIER

(PAUSSINIBYI SPRAYI)

THE JOB ISN'T FUN

BUT IT'S STILL SO IMPORTANT

DISINFECTING ALL

PPE LE PEW

(Mesmellit aromasini)

EACH CHOICE SEEMS TO MEAN

BLACK OR WHITE CONSEQUENCES

CORONAVIRUS

DAILY BALANCE
(Salientaia hanioni)

SHELVES EMPTY; STORES FULL
IT'S QUITE THE BALANCING ACT
SHOPPING IS THE WORST

SELF RELIANT
(Sourdoughnite bakiti)

AT NIGHT, WITHOUT YEAST
SHE'S WORKING UNDER THE STARS
PUFF, PUFFING THE LUMP

STANDBACK DIAMOND BACK
(CROTALUS SCARIFORMEE)

SHAKE, RATTLE AND ROLL

BANDANAS WORN NOW SCARE ME

SOCIAL DISTANCING

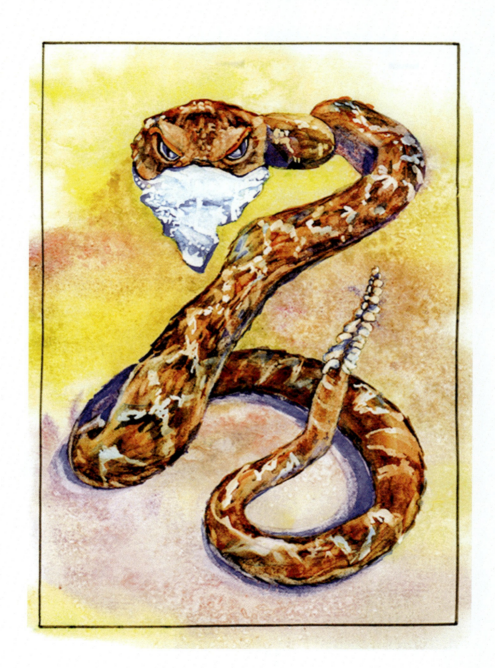

FURLOUGHED

(Equus reallisadnow)

SINCE FURLOUGH BEGAN

THERE IS TIME TO WATCH THE MOON

THE VANISHED PAYROLL

RESTRICTIONS RATTLED

(Geococcys noairi)

SUDDENLY STOPPING

TAKES OF THE HOT CLOTH TO BREATHE

HATED MASK FATIGUE

TOPI SHARING T.P.
(Damaliscus sharitwidus)

A FORTUNATE ONE

SHARES A PRECIOUS, KIND TREASURE

PANIC-BOUGHT 2-PLY

GETTING SWABBED
(ERINACEUS SCAREDTASWABBI)

SMALL, SCARED, BUT PREPARED

GAG TESTING FOR HIDDEN THREATS

A LONG, LONG, THIN SWAB

HERE I GO FLAMINGO

(Phoeni rulesigonri)

FEATHERS A FLUTTER

DENYING AWAY WARNINGS

SHE'S OFF TO SPRING BREAK

DECKED OUT

(Iguannali deckedouti"

CINCI DE MAYO

FIESTA WITH US ON ZOOM

CELEBRATE SAFELY

FEELING OSTRICHIZED?

(Struthio ignorihygieni)

ALONE AND SCRAGGLY

PERSONAL HYGIENE LONG GONE

QUARANTINE JUST STINKS

33

TRAIL SNAIL
(Achatinodidea helofadae)

SEARCHING THE LONG TRAIL

RETRACING EACH LEAD SLOWLY

CONTACT TRACINGS

CORONA = RACOON

(Pronomen rearrangee)

Always hand washing

Intelligently wears masks

Common courtesy

SHAMED

(Dendrocoughonus major)

COUGH-SHAMED, EMBARRASSED

HE SPREADS HIS WINGS, FLIES AWAY

SELF ISOLATING

THE PREDICAMENT
(Equusgot agrievancei)

BROTHERS BY CHANCE MEET

ONE WITH, ONE WITHOUT A MASK

FEAR AND DISTRUST LOOM

POOR BEAR
(Ursus isolationishe)

AFTER THE COLD HUNT

THE SCENT OF SEALS ON THE ICE

HUNGER SUFFERER

EATING OUT

(Vermilingua tasterouti)

DINING OUT TODAY

HARD TO EAT WEARING A MASK

TASTEBUDS IN CONTROL

LIKE A CHAMELEON YEARS

(Chamilldia quaranteendme)

INDEPENDENT EYES

WANDER HIGH AND LOW ALL DAY

SOLITUDE IS SAD

PUZZLED
(Alines socofuusii)

FACT OR ALL FAKE NEWS

COHORTS BLAMING SHIFTS DAILY

RACIST COMMENTS THRIVE

CODE YELLOW
(Apis millifreea)

BUZZING FROM THE HIVE

SEEKING STICKY, SWEET NECTAR

FRANTIC TO BE OUT

BAT TO THE FUTURE

(CHIROPTERA WHENGOI)

THIS LIFE UPSIDE DOWN

MIGHT LEAD SOME TO DEPRESSION

HIGH ANXIETY

EMERGING LOCKDOWN
(CARETTA HOUDINIS)

EMERGING QUICKLY

AND LEAVING CAUTION BEHIND

AN OPTIMIST TRUE

GENERATION RESILIENT

(HOPEOVRFEAR GENEROUS)

BORN INTO CRISIS

ADAPTABLE RESILIENT

THE GLOBAL COURSE CHANGED

AUTHORIZED DISTRIBUTOR

(Endless whirler)

ON SCHEDULE TODAY A

DYNAMIC SOLUTION

VACCINATION BLITZ

FUTURE
(Boobysula saundernowa)

ONE DAY THIS WILL END

I WILL THEN WADDLE MASK FREE

WITH IMMUNITY

TEAM EFFORT
(Wiseones arwe)

RESILIENT ARE YOU

DOING YOUR ABSOLUTE BEST

FOR THE QUARAN TEAM

LINDA KOHLER BARNES

Linda is an artist who works in multiple mediums.
She chose watercolor for this unique covid experience.

Hopefully all viewers will be drawn to their own
moments through this unprecidented crisis.

Her paintings and Haiku have delighted and appealed
to people of all ages and have helped address their
fears and evoked a new confidence and personal
adaptation to our "New Normal".

Linda was born and continues to live in Utah, USA.
She is married with children and lovely grandchildren.

She graduated from the University of Utah with
a BFA degree and has won prestigous awards
in most of her varied mediums. She has been an
educator most of her adult life and retired from long
tenure as an instructor at Utah Valley University.

Her fondest wish is that you will find here
some enjoyment that will help you through
these challenging times.

With grateful thanks to her beloved Ted

Printed in the United States
by Baker & Taylor Publisher Services